Arnold Palmer
GOLF ACADEMY
Golf Journal

*A Personal Handbook of Practice,
Performance, and Progress*

GOLF ACADEMY

TRIUMPH
BOOKS
CHICAGO

Acknowledgment

A special thank you to Brad Brewer,
Director of the Arnold Palmer Golf
Academy, for providing the information
contained in this journal.

Golf Training Systems, Inc., is dedicated to providing golfers of all abilities with the proper tools and educational materials to make the learning process more efficient and more enjoyable than ever before. Our name says it all…when it comes to golf, we know our business.

Cover photo, courtesy of "Play Great Golf." Photo, page 1 courtesy of Mike Lloyd/*The Oregonian*. Photos, pages 7, 79, 89, & 95 courtesy of "Play Great Golf." Photos, pages 35, 43, 57, 61, & 71 courtesy of the Arnold Palmer Collection. Text, pages 49, 50, 54, & 55 courtesy of Dr. James Loehr, LGE, Sports Science, Inc. Back cover photo, courtesy of Mesquite Vistas / Oasis Golf Club.

Printed in the United States of America.

This book is available in quantity at special discounts for your group or organization. For more information, contact:

Triumph Books
644 South Clark Street
Chicago, Illinois 60605
(312) 939-3330 Fax (312) 663-3557

Book and cover design by Mulligan + Mulligan Design.

ISBN 1-57243-172-5

Contents

GOLF ACADEMY

My views on the game aren't ones that have been molded slowly through years of playing and practicing. They are based on simple fundamentals taught to me by my father, Deacon Palmer, who was head pro and greenkeeper at the Latrobe Country Club in western Pennsylvania, where I grew up.

Pap believed in keeping the game as simple as possible. He felt that if a player mastered simple fundamentals, then his swing and his entire game would develop naturally.

The one thing my father always stressed, though, was practice. To him, the brain could learn the basics of golf from reading or watching, but practice taught the body what they were. He'd be the first to point out that nothing, not even a book by his son, could take the place of getting out and hitting golf balls. It's how I learned, and how you should as well.

If you possess the burning desire to play great golf, along with a willingness to work hard at your game, you'll discover the secrets that I learned from Pap long ago, that playing great golf is not as difficult as it might appear, and that the game is a lifelong joy to play when you find out how easy it actually can be.

Arnold Palmer

My Philosophy to Playing Great Golf

"I can't tell you how much I appreciate what the game has done for me. I look at the people I've met and the associations I've made through golf. I met my wife Winnie through golf. I can't give enough to golf. If I had more, I'd give more. Everything I have I owe to golf."

ARNOLD PALMER

I am confident that your journey to success and fun with golf will be assisted and enhanced by following the suggested practice and training programs within this wonderful golf journal. The *Arnold Palmer Golf Academy Golf Journal* also gives you a library of your fondest golf memories and accomplishments from your adventures on the links.

Arnold Palmer's Four Areas of Golf Instruction

MASTER THE FUNDAMENTALS

- Grip
- Address
- Steady head
- One-piece takeaway
- Acceleration

PRACTICE LIKE A PRO

- The point of practice
- Make practice fun
- Always hit to a target
- Mental toughness skills
- Pre-shot routine

SCORING ZONE

- Putting
- Chipping
- Pitching
- Bunkers

COURSE STRATEGY

- Going for broke, bailing out, playing safe
- Matching your strategy with your skills
- Know your game and your course down to the yard
- Rules and etiquette

The Swing as a Whole

The swing should be looked at as a whole. The key to developing this whole-swing motion depends on the mastery of a few, simple fundamentals. Once you understand and employ them, the swing happens naturally and automatically, with no conscious effort on your part.

There is no such thing as one correct swing that every golfer should try to imitate. In fact, the "perfect swing" myth keeps many golfers from playing great golf.

Instead, every swing should be as individual as the player himself. You may know two friends who both hit the ball well with two radically different-looking swings. That's why, although good swings share certain basics, in many ways they can vary tremendously.

If you still don't believe me, look at the swings of some of the top golfers on the Professional Golfers Association Tour over the years. Compare Jack Nicklaus to Lee Trevino to Johnny Miller. You'll see that very different-looking swings can be equally effective in achieving excellent golf shots. Despite having different body shapes, varying body turns, more or less wrist action, and different ball flight, these three pros produce the shots it takes to play great golf. Explain that, if you will, if you're an advocate of the "perfect swing" theory.

The reason these different-looking swings have produced such outstanding results lies in the fundamentals that are the basis for all good golf swings—the same fundamentals that my father taught me. Ironically, they often are overlooked in the quest for the perfect swing. Although most golfers believe that a uniform technique is necessary, they often ignore the very elements that actually are uniform among good swings.

Just Five Fundamentals

These are the five fundamentals inherent in all good golf swings. You should try to incorporate them into your swing.

FUNDAMENTAL ONE: THE GRIP

The way you hold the club. There is one correct grip; good golf is impossible without it. (These instructions are for right-handed golfers.)

Left Hand

- The club lays across your palm from the fat pad between the knuckles of your left index finger to the base of fat pad at the bottom of your palm.

- The left thumb is parallel to the axis of the shaft.

- The end of the club protrudes approximately 1/4" from the pad; no more for full shots.

- A "V" is formed by the thumb and the index finger points to the right shoulder.

Right Hand

- The club lays across the bottom knuckle of your middle and ring fingers.

- The left thumb is under the cup of your right palm; its tip touches the fat pad at the base of the index finger.

- A "V" is formed by the thumb and the index finger points to the right shoulder.

- The base of the thumb and the base of the index finger touch from the bottom out to the thumb knuckle, then they separate.

Widely Used Grips

- The Ten Finger or Baseball Grip requires all ten fingers on the club. This grip is recommended for beginners.

- The Interlocking Grip is when the forefinger of the left hand and the little finger of your right hand interlock. Novices upward with small hands should use this grip.

- The Overlapping or Vardon Grip is formed when the little finger of the right hand overlaps the left forefinger and rests in the channel between your left index and middle fingers. This grip is recommended for novices upward with medium to large hands. (It is named for a famous English golf champion who actually began playing the overlap style grip in the early 1900's.)

Grip Pressure

- Medium to light pressure is applied to the grip by the last three fingers of your left hand and the middle two fingers of your right hand.

FUNDAMENTAL TWO: THE ADDRESS

The relationship between your posture, alignment, and ball position that creates a well-balanced athletic address position.

Posture

- Feet should be shoulder width apart measured from the outside of your shoulders to the mid-point of your heels.

- Keep feet slightly toed out.

- Thrust hip girdles backward.

- Bend forward from the waist keeping the lower back straight.

- Distribute weight equally from left to right and between the balls of your feet and heels.

- Flex knees slightly for a springy, light, athletic balance.

Alignment

- Driver through five-iron square stance: feet, knees, hips, and shoulders are parallel to line of flight. (Toe line is approximately 7-10 yards left of target.)

- Six-iron through wedge-open stance: left foot is pulled back slightly from a square stance and feet are slightly narrowed from longer club stance. This stance promotes a shorter backswing for control and a descending angle of attack for your backspin.

Ball Position

- A ball is played two inches inside the left heel with respect to the line of flight of all clubs.

- An open stance with short irons makes the ball appear farther back in the stance, but this is an optical illusion.

- Uniform ball position is necessary to attain square clubface and true loft of all clubs.

- From a front view, the club and left arm form a straight line.

FUNDAMENTAL THREE: THE TAKEAWAY

The path of the club and your arms during the start of the swing.

- Your hands, arms, and shoulders should take the club back as a unit for at least two feet.

- The straight line formed by your left arm and the club is retained.

- Keep legs relaxed to allow them to respond to the action of your upper body.

- The club is started straight back from the ball for at least two feet to establish proper direction of swing.

- The club is started back smoothly to establish smooth acceleration.

Proper execution of the takeaway lets all the parts of your body move together; achieving maximum efficiency and establishing a wide radius for your swing.

FUNDAMENTAL FOUR: THE STEADY HEAD

The position of the head during the swing.

- The club is swung in a circle with the head at the center.
- Any head motion on the backswing must be followed by an equal and opposite movement on the forward swing to attain solid contact.
- Do not "keep your eye on the ball"; watching the ball can cause the head to experience severe movement.
- Do not "keep your head down"; your head must be allowed to release after impact so as not to hinder acceleration.

FUNDAMENTAL FIVE: ACCELERATION

The increasing speed at which the clubhead moves through the ball.

- Acceleration must be smooth and its tempo must match your temperament as a player.
- Smoothness is started during the takeaway.
- The club continues back until it reaches the point at which it must be forced to go any further.
- The club is accelerated smoothly from the top by all parts of the body working together around a steady head.
- If tension is present in the swing or if any part of the body resists the flow of the motion, then smooth acceleration is impossible.

It is impossible to put too much emphasis on the value of these five elements. If you work to master each of them, the rest of your swing will take care of itself. Your individual swing will automatically develop, based on physical ability, age, body type, and style of play.

The results will come shining forth in your game. You'll enjoy hitting the ball more because you'll be hitting it where you want it to go with maximum power. Forget about all of the technical questions and theories that the analytic players use.

It's my firm belief that if every serious golfer took the time and made the effort to learn fully these five swing fundamentals, there wouldn't be anyone shooting above 90.

Practice Like a Pro

"There is no such individual as a born golfer."

BEN HOGAN

The Point of Practice

Practicing like a pro is more than just beating balls. Each shot is thought out and has a purpose.

The goal in golf is not to build a picture-perfect swing but to build a functional swing, and more importantly, a repeatable swing. If you can't swing at the ball the same way twice, you aren't going to have much luck at this game.

That's why practicing is so important. It conditions the muscles and the body to make the proper swing moves until they become automatic and reflexive, or grooved. At that point, you can perform them without any thought when you're on the course. Players often get discouraged because they tackle too much at once and end up not getting much of a handle on anything.

When practicing, remember to:

- Make the practice tee the workshop where you build a sound swing or adjust one that needs fixing.

- Take your time between shots and really concentrate on ingraining the proper fundamentals into each and every swing.

- Devote each practice session to one or two specific goals.

When learning the fundamentals, the proper feels must first be felt through drills and exercises. During this period, new feels will usually produce erratic and unsatisfactory ball flight, so ball flight must be ignored. It is essential that drilling be done as often as possible. For this reason, those who cannot get to the range every day are strongly urged to modify the drills and do them at home every day for ten or fifteen minutes.

After working on the new fundamentals for a while, the swing starts to feel natural and some solid shots will be struck. Once solid contact has been attained, good direction will soon follow. This initial period of learning is one in which the new moves are all made consciously. Until these feels become ingrained in the subconscious portion of the mind, they will produce little improvement on the golf course. During this time, some great shots will be hit on the course, usually followed by quite mediocre ones, and the score will not improve. Only when these fundamentals are firmly embedded in the subconscious, and all remains of the old swing are removed, will consistent performance on the golf course appear.

ALWAYS HIT TO A TARGET

- The most important part of a golf shot is that it goes where you want it to go.

- It's therefore especially important always to have a target in mind when hitting practice balls.

- Don't get into the habit of just swinging away and trying to make good contact.

SPACING SESSIONS OUT

I'd strongly recommend spacing out your practice sessions throughout the week, rather than putting in one or two long ones. You'll usually get too fatigued by trying to practice for too long, which often leads to picking up bad and lazy habits.

MAKE PRACTICE FUN

The most important thing you can bring with you to the practice tee is the right attitude. Make practice fun, not a drudgery. If you look at it as boring time spent hacking away at balls, then that's what it will be. If you approach practice with the attitude that it will help you improve your playing ability and lead to lower scores, you'll find your practice much more productive.

I'll often pretend I'm playing an entire round from tee to green on one of my favorite courses, hitting every drive and approach shot from the first hole to the eighteenth. My point is that, with the help of the right attitude and your imagination, your practice sessions can be more enjoyable and as a result, more productive.

So stop wasting time. Go out to your workshop and get to work. You can then look forward—realistically—to a better swing and lower scores.

NUTRITIONAL GUIDELINES

A player who eats better will perform better. Pay special attention to what you eat before practicing and competing.

BEFORE YOUR WORKOUT

Consume foods high in carbohydrates during the twenty-four hours before a workout or competition.

Good choices include:

- Fruit
- Vegetables
- Salads
- Potatoes
- Rice
- Pasta
- Turkey
- Whole Grain Breads
- Oatmeal
- Cereals
- Plain Yogurt
- Egg Whites
- Chicken
- Fish

Consume less:

- Butter
- Margarine
- Mayonnaise
- Egg Yolks
- Red Meat
- Ice Cream
- Candy
- Doughnuts
- Danishes
- Cookies
- Creamy Salad Dressings
- Fried Foods
- Chocolate

DURING YOUR WORKOUT

- An athlete tires after one to three hours of continuous exercise due to carbohydrate depletion.

- To maintain a healthy level of carbohydrates, you need to drink eight ounces of sports drink (5-8% carbohydrate solution) every fifteen minutes.

- Carbohydrate feeding can delay fatigue from thirty minutes to an hour.

AFTER YOUR WORKOUT

- It is crucial to replenish carbohydrates during the first two hours after exercise.

- Athletes who train for one to two hours daily may need 2000-2400 calories (500-600 grams) from carbohydrates to replace muscle glycogen stores in their daily diet.

Golf Flexibility Exercises

These exercises can be used prior to both practice and competition. They will loosen up the body for an overall better and safer performance.

Do stretching gently and hold the position, no bouncing, abrupt forcing, or jerking. Warm-up before stretching with some light jogging in place or jumping jacks.

1. Lace fingers together and extend hands upwards; hold for fifteen seconds. (Hands, fingers, and shoulders)

2. Place hands and arms behind your head; hold for fifteen seconds on each side. (Neck)

3. Holding a golf club or towel behind your neck, stretch your back; hold for fifteen seconds. (Shoulders)

4. With feet flat on the floor, twist and place your hands on the wall; hold for thirty seconds on each side. (Hips and obliques)

5. Keep the heel of your rear leg on the floor; hold for thirty seconds on each leg. (Lower leg)

6. Grab your foot with the opposing hand and pull toward the buttocks until the stretch is felt; hold for fifteen seconds on each leg. (Quadriceps)

7. Put your elbow behind your head and gently pull toward the center of the back until the stretch is felt; hold for fifteen seconds on each arm. (Shoulders)

8. Form a tight ball position by clasping your legs to your chest and rock back and forth about eight to ten times. (Back)

9. Keeping shoulders flat, swing your knee to the floor until the stretch is felt and hold for fifteen seconds on each leg. (Iliotibial band)

10. Sitting upright, place feet together and push gently down on knees until stretch is felt and hold for thirty seconds. (Groin)

11. Grab ankle or shin and hold for thirty seconds on each leg. (Hamstrings)

12. Sit backward toward your heels until the stretch is felt and hold for twenty seconds. (Wrists)

© PGA *Manual of Golf*, Courtesy PGA of America

"Always bear in mind that your own resolution to succeed is more important than any other thing."
Abraham Lincoln

DATE	PRACTICE FOCUS	RESULTS

Practice Routine

Establish a pattern for practice.

Use these charts to record the days that you practiced, what you focused on, and what was achieved.

SUMMARY

_____

_____

_____

_____

_____

Practice
Routine

DATE	PRACTICE FOCUS	RESULTS

SUMMARY

_____

_____

_____

_____

_____

DATE	PRACTICE FOCUS	RESULTS

Practice Routine

Establish a pattern for practice.

Use these charts to record the days that you practiced, what you focused on, and what was achieved.

SUMMARY

Practice Routine

DATE	PRACTICE FOCUS	RESULTS

SUMMARY

_____

_____

_____

_____

_____

DATE	PRACTICE FOCUS	RESULTS

Practice Routine

Establish a pattern for practice.

Use these charts to record the days that you practiced, what you focused on, and what was achieved.

SUMMARY

_____

_____

_____

_____

_____

Practice
Notes

Practice
Notes

The P.A.R. Evaluation—Rating Your Progress

The P.A.R. system and the P.A.R. chart were developed for instructors of the Arnold Palmer Golf Academy to rate their pupils' progress. You can use the Academy's system for self-evaluation in the five main areas covered by this chart—or ask your teaching professional to fill out a "report card" to help you monitor improvements in each specific area of your game.

I.   FIVE FUNDAMENTALS: IF YOU WORK TO MASTER THE FUNDAMENTALS, THE REST OF YOUR SWING WILL TAKE CARE OF ITSELF.

   A.   Grip: Pick the grip that works for you: ten finger, interlocking or overlapping (Vardon). Grip pressure should be medium to light.

   B.   Address: Check the distance between your feet, hip thrust, waist bend, and balance. Set alignment according to the length of the club and use an open stance with left foot pulled back slightly. Place the ball two inches inside the left heel. From a front view, the club and left arm form a straight line.

   C.   Takeaway: Let all parts of your body move together to achieve maximum efficiency and to establish a wide radius for your swing.

   D.   Keep your head steady! Any head motion on the backswing must be followed by an equal and opposite movement on the downswing to attain solid contact.

   E.   Acceleration: Must match your playing tempo.

II.   PRACTICE LIKE A PRO: PRACTICING PROFESSIONALLY IS MORE THAN JUST HITTING BALLS.

   A.   Organized schedule: The only way to develop a functional, repeatable swing is with practice. The practice tee should be a workshop for building and repairing.

   B.   Fundamentals: Concentrate on the five basics for each shot.

   C.   Preshot: Develop consistent preshot routines and stick with them. Always hit toward a target.

   D.   Visualization: Set specific goals for each practice.

III. SCORING ZONE: TO SCORE WELL, YOU NEED A SOLID SHORT GAME. AIM FOR CONSISTENCY AND ACCURACY FROM A VARIETY OF LIES AND CONDITIONS. PRACTICE EACH OF THE NECESSARY STROKES:

A. Pitching

B. Chipping

C. Sand shots

D. Putting

IV. COURSE STRATEGY: TO PLAY WELL, YOU NEED A PLAN. THINK BEFORE YOU HIT AND TAILOR YOUR COURSE STRATEGY TO YOUR INDIVIDUAL GAME.

A. Course Management: Use recovery skills—while walking to your next shot, learn to relax. Preshot analysis includes noting yardage, wind conditions, lie, etc.

B. This enables you to make a confident club selection.

V. SHOT MAKING: PRACTICE SHOT MAKING AT THE RANGE SO WHEN A TOUGH SITUATION ARRIVES, YOU'LL BE MENTALLY AND PHYSICALLY PREPARED TO PLAY YOUR BEST GAME.

P.A.R.
Progress
Analysis
Report

_____

Date

NOTES & COMMENTS

I. FIVE FUNDAMENTALS	
A. THE GRIP	
B. ADDRESS POSTURE & ALIGNMENT	
C. TAKE-AWAY	
D. SWING HEAD	
E. ACCELERATION	
II. PRACTICE LIKE A PRO	
A. ORGANIZED SCHEDULE	
B. FUNDAMENTALS	
C. PRE-SHOT	
D. VISUALIZATION	
III. SCORING ZONE	
A. PITCHING	
B. CHIPPING	
C. SAND SHOTS	
D. PUTTING	
IV. COURSE STRATEGY	
A. COURSE MANAGEMENT	
B. CONFIDENCE	
V. SHOT MAKING	
VI. MISCELLANEOUS COMMENTS	

SUMMARY

_____

_____

_____

_____

_____

_____

_____

NOTES & COMMENTS

P.A.R.
Progress Analysis Report

_____
Date

I. FIVE FUNDAMENTALS	
A. THE GRIP	
B. ADDRESS POSTURE & ALIGNMENT	
C. TAKE-AWAY	
D. SWING HEAD	
E. ACCELERATION	
II. PRACTICE LIKE A PRO	
A. ORGANIZED SCHEDULE	
B. FUNDAMENTALS	
C. PRE-SHOT	
D. VISUALIZATION	
III. SCORING ZONE	
A. PITCHING	
B. CHIPPING	
C. SAND SHOTS	
D. PUTTING	
IV. COURSE STRATEGY	
A. COURSE MANAGEMENT	
B. CONFIDENCE	
V. SHOT MAKING	
VI. MISCELLANEOUS COMMENTS	

SUMMARY

_____

_____

_____

_____

_____

_____

_____

P.A.R.
*Progress
Analysis
Report*

_____

Date

NOTES & COMMENTS

I. FIVE FUNDAMENTALS	
A. THE GRIP	
B. ADDRESS POSTURE & ALIGNMENT	
C. TAKE-AWAY	
D. SWING HEAD	
E. ACCELERATION	
II. PRACTICE LIKE A PRO	
A. ORGANIZED SCHEDULE	
B. FUNDAMENTALS	
C. PRE-SHOT	
D. VISUALIZATION	
III. SCORING ZONE	
A. PITCHING	
B. CHIPPING	
C. SAND SHOTS	
D. PUTTING	
IV. COURSE STRATEGY	
A. COURSE MANAGEMENT	
B. CONFIDENCE	
V. SHOT MAKING	
VI. MISCELLANEOUS COMMENTS	

SUMMARY

_____

_____

_____

_____

_____

_____

_____

_____

NOTES & COMMENTS

P.A.R.
Progress Analysis Report

Date

I. FIVE FUNDAMENTALS	
A. THE GRIP	
B. ADDRESS POSTURE & ALIGNMENT	
C. TAKE-AWAY	
D. SWING HEAD	
E. ACCELERATION	
II. PRACTICE LIKE A PRO	
A. ORGANIZED SCHEDULE	
B. FUNDAMENTALS	
C. PRE-SHOT	
D. VISUALIZATION	
III. SCORING ZONE	
A. PITCHING	
B. CHIPPING	
C. SAND SHOTS	
D. PUTTING	
IV. COURSE STRATEGY	
A. COURSE MANAGEMENT	
B. CONFIDENCE	
V. SHOT MAKING	
VI. MISCELLANEOUS COMMENTS	

SUMMARY

_____

_____

_____

_____

_____

_____

_____

_____

Lesson
Notes

PROBLEMS

SOLUTIONS

_____

Instructor

_____

Date

NOTES

PROGRESS REPORTS

PROBLEMS

_____

_____

_____

_____

_____

_____

_____

_____

_____

_____

_____

SOLUTIONS

_____

_____

_____

_____

_____

_____

_____

_____

_____

_____

_____

Lesson Notes

In order to best profit from the time spent taking lessons, take notes on each lesson—what you learned, weaknesses and strengths, practice patterns and tips.

_____

Instructor

_____

Date

NOTES

_____

_____

_____

_____

_____

_____

PROGRESS REPORTS

_____

_____

_____

_____

_____

Lesson Notes

Instructor
_____

Date
_____

PROBLEMS

SOLUTIONS

NOTES

PROGRESS REPORTS

PROBLEMS

SOLUTIONS

Lesson Notes

In order to best profit from the time spent taking lessons, take notes on each lesson—what you learned, weaknesses and strengths, practice patterns and tips.

_____

Instructor

_____

Date

NOTES

_____
_____
_____
_____
_____
_____

PROGRESS REPORTS

_____
_____
_____
_____
_____
_____

Lesson Notes

Instructor

Date

PROBLEMS

SOLUTIONS

NOTES

PROGRESS REPORTS

PROBLEMS

SOLUTIONS

Lesson Notes

In order to best profit from the time spent taking lessons, take notes on each lesson—what you learned, weaknesses and strengths, practice patterns and tips.

Instructor

Date

NOTES

PROGRESS REPORTS

Lesson Notes

Instructor

Date

PROBLEMS

SOLUTIONS

NOTES

PROGRESS REPORTS

PROBLEMS

SOLUTIONS

Lesson Notes

In order to best profit from the time spent taking lessons, take notes on each lesson—what you learned, weaknesses and strengths, practice patterns and tips.

_____

Instructor

_____

Date

NOTES

PROGRESS REPORTS

Dreams, Goals, and Actions

"A golfer can't dictate what his opponents shoot. He can't wave his arms or tackle a playing partner who's getting ready to putt. But he can always reach within himself to bring out the best in his battle against the laws of physics and par."

ARNOLD PALMER

Goal Setting

Your goal setting and how you break down your goals is very important to maximizing your potential in tournament play.

Good goals are performance goals, things you can control, important things that will make you become a better golfer. They should be based on overcoming weaknesses in specific areas. Focus on three or four things to do to overcome these weaknesses for the long term. This will help build confidence even when you don't score your best. Set daily, weekly, and long term goals, and monitor your progress!

Poor goals are ones that really don't affect performance and are not in your control: win the tournament, score, how am I playing right now, etc. These can be very dangerous and break your confidence if they are not reached.

LONG-TERM AND SHORT-TERM GOALS

It is important for the serious golfer to have both short- and long-term goals. Short-term goals should include a set number of at-home drills each day, a set number of days to practice at the range each week, and an organized routine for each practice. Long-term goals are usually performance oriented; lowering the handicap by five shots in a year, or breaking eighty, or hitting 70% of the fairways for a month.

How well the long-term goals are met will be determined by two factors: how realistic the long-term goal, and how faithful you are in adhering to your short-term goals. Diligence, perseverance, concentration, and patience are necessary if you are to "practice like a pro."

Key ingredients when considering your goals:

- Make certain your goals are your own. Only you can define and measure your success.

- Be certain your goals benefit yourself and others.

- Set your goals big enough and high enough.

- Always make sure your goals are stated in the positive.

"The price of greatness is responsibility."
Winston Churchill

Keep in mind that you should set attainable goals that can become part of your regular routine. With consistent practice, these goals will help you to reach your full potential.

Break down your game into strengths and weaknesses. Know how many putts you score per round, fairways hit, etc. After analyzing your game, you will have a much clearer idea on how and where to focus your goal-setting.

Use the Ladder to Success chart as a way to map out your journey toward achieving your goals. Begin by targeting where you want to end up, your ultimate goal. Compare your present skill level with the desired model or level you hope to reach. Write down your strengths and weaknesses. List the areas you need to improve upon the most. Develop a weekly practice routine that includes all areas of your game, devoting more time to your weakest points.

For example, if your goal is to improve your swing, start your goal-setting with the five fundamentals. First examine your grip. Choose the most comfortable grip. Make sure your grasp on the club is light to medium. Work on holding the club correctly.

Then look at your address. Watch your stance, line your feet up correctly. Visualize yourself standing over the ball with your waist bent and hips thrust. Is your takeaway a fluid motion? If not, isolate the problem areas and focus on fixing them.

Keep your head still. Concentrate on maintaining your address. Are you rushing through your swing? Note your acceleration; it should match your playing tempo.

Following your daily commitments will lead to the development of a better golf game. Going after the challenges you set for yourself will make you a stronger player and a more prepared competitor.

Ladder to Success

Target Goal: List the goal which you want to accomplish.

Focus on the most important aspect of your game that needs to improve so that you can advance to the next rung of the ladder.

Daily action is your commitment to work on the skills that need improvement in order to accomplish your desired goal.

TARGET GOAL:

_____

_____

_____

_____

RUNG 1 DATE: _____

GOAL: _____

_____

DAILY ACTIONS TOWARD SKILL DEVELOPMENT:

1. _____ 4. _____

2. _____ 5. _____

3. _____ 6. _____

RUNG 2 DATE: _____

GOAL: _____

_____

DAILY ACTIONS TOWARD SKILL DEVELOPMENT:

1. _____ 4. _____

2. _____ 5. _____

3. _____ 6. _____

RUNG 3 DATE: _____

GOAL: _____

_____

DAILY ACTIONS TOWARD SKILL DEVELOPMENT:

1. _____ 4. _____

2. _____ 5. _____

3. _____ 6. _____

RUNG **4** DATE:

GOAL:

DAILY ACTIONS TOWARD SKILL DEVELOPMENT:

1.   4.

2.   5.

3.   6.

RUNG **5** DATE:

GOAL:

DAILY ACTIONS TOWARD SKILL DEVELOPMENT:

1.   4.

2.   5.

3.   6.

SUMMARY

RUNG **5** ☑

RUNG **4** ☑

RUNG **3** ☑

RUNG **2** ☑

RUNG **1** ☑

Ladder to Success

Target Goal: List the goal which you want to accomplish.

Focus on the most important aspect of your game that needs to improve so that you can advance to the next rung of the ladder.

Daily action is your commitment to work on the skills that need improvement in order to accomplish your desired goal.

TARGET GOAL:

_____

_____

_____

_____

_____

RUNG 1 DATE: _____

GOAL: _____

_____

DAILY ACTIONS TOWARD SKILL DEVELOPMENT:

1. _____ 4. _____

2. _____ 5. _____

3. _____ 6. _____

RUNG 2 DATE: _____

GOAL: _____

_____

DAILY ACTIONS TOWARD SKILL DEVELOPMENT:

1. _____ 4. _____

2. _____ 5. _____

3. _____ 6. _____

RUNG 3 DATE: _____

GOAL: _____

_____

DAILY ACTIONS TOWARD SKILL DEVELOPMENT:

1. _____ 4. _____

2. _____ 5. _____

3. _____ 6. _____

RUNG **4** DATE: _____

GOAL: _____

_____

DAILY ACTIONS TOWARD SKILL DEVELOPMENT:

1. _____   4. _____

2. _____   5. _____

3. _____   6. _____

RUNG **5** DATE: _____

GOAL: _____

_____

DAILY ACTIONS TOWARD SKILL DEVELOPMENT:

1. _____   4. _____

2. _____   5. _____

3. _____   6. _____

SUMMARY

_____

_____

_____

_____

_____

_____

_____

_____

_____

_____

_____

RUNG **5** ☑

RUNG **4** ☑

RUNG **3** ☑

RUNG **2** ☑

RUNG **1** ☑

The Mental Game

"Golf is a game of inches, the most important are those between the ears."

ARNOLD PALMER

The Making of a Winner

Attitude... *positive and mentally tough*

Responsible... *for own actions*

Noble... *high morals and standards*

Organized... *time management and routines*

Leader... *by example and direction; inspires others*

Discipline... *self control, consistency*

Desire... *want, need, dream; fuel for success*

Perseverance... *stay focused*

Athlete... *mental and physical toughness*

Legend... *dedicated to tradition*

Modesty... *feet on the ground*

Energy... *fueled by desire and positive attitude*

Resilience... *flexibility and ability to adapt; recovers quickly from mistakes or loss; being competitive*

Becoming a Great Competitor

- Talent is a gift (God-given and self-nurtured)
- Learned skills (hard work, repetition, practice)
- Physical skills (diet, exercise, sleep, swing fundamentals)
- Emotional control (positive attitude, visualization, thinking)
- Ideal Performance State or IPS (confident, relaxed, calm, energized positive emotion, challenged, focused, alert, automatic, instinctive, fun, and enjoyment)
- Expectations (self, coach, family, media, friends)
- Real self vs. performer self (disciplined thinkers)

Learning to Visualize

You probably have heard that playing good golf is mostly mental, and it is. Clear thinking leads to good decisions on strategy. That's a key element in scoring well.

Another equally important mental aspect of the game is visualization, the process of imagining what the shot you are about to play will feel and look like before you play it. This valuable asset will serve you well anywhere on the course, from the tee to the scoring zone to trouble play.

Before you hit any shot, imagine everything about it. The feel of the club in your hands as you grip it, the backswing and the downswing, impact. Then imagine the ball flying to your target and finishing exactly as planned.

Visualizing the shot from start to finish helps activate your muscle memory for playing the shot you want to play. It's especially helpful in a pressure situation. Visualizing the result you want also blocks out negative thoughts.

"We tend to get what we expect."
Norman Vincent Peale

Even if this is the first time you have formally heard about visualizing a golf shot before hitting it, you probably have done it without realizing it. Think about one of your favorite par-3 holes—one where you always feel you'll hit the green. Every time you step up to the tee, memories of past good shots come flooding back. You "see" the ball arching toward the green and automatically "feel" that good 7-iron swing. You gain such confidence from thinking about it that you can't wait to do it again. That's what good visualization can trigger on every shot.

The more you practice visualization, the better you'll get at it, and the more it will help your play. If you're like me, when you aren't playing golf, you like to relax by thinking about your game. The next time you do, try playing a few holes in your imagination.

Picture yourself on the tee of your favorite par four on a beautiful windless morning. You tee up the ball and survey the situation, picking out a landing area. Make a good swing—crack—and it flies straight toward your target.

Now for your second shot. It's on a good lie and 150 yards from the pin, which is tucked behind a bunker guarding the right front of the green. The air is calm, so you take your 5-iron and aim for the middle of the green playing your normal fade. Take your grip, address, swing—contact—and the ball flies first toward the center of the green, then drifts right before softly settling pin high, about ten feet from the flag.

Finally, your birdie putt. It looks as if it will break a little right to left, so you'll play it about a ball-width outside the right edge. It's slightly uphill, and the grain is against you, so be a little firmer with it. Take your stance, get comfortable, be confident and stroke. Feels good. Nice roll. Bingo!

Try it the next time your mind drifts off toward golf. It's good mental practice, it's fun, and you'll find you rarely get into trouble or make a bogey. Talk about improving your game.

"Roller coaster emotions produce roller coaster competitors."

Jim E. Loehr

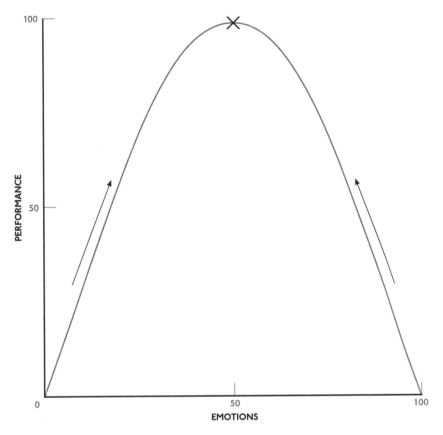

Controlling your emotions

Anger is tanking it!

Positive Emotions Run the Show

Being able to control your emotions is the key to peak performance and mental toughness. Achieving 100% performance can be done by finding that balance point with your emotions; somewhere between overly excited and not having a care in the world. We can balance our emotions by doing the following:

Over emotional

- Slow down everything
- Breathe deeply and exhale
- Focus on one shot at a time
- Laugh and have fun

Under emotional

- Become more active and aggressive
- Think about your goals
- Get creative and visual
- Recall your best performance

Ideal Performance State (IPS)

The list below is a consensus of thoughts and feelings taken from the minds of golf's great champions as they explain their best performances.

A. Soft and slow

B. Relaxed-no muscle tension

C. Motion-full and free, swinging of the clubhead through the ball

D. Swing felt long and slow

E. I was happy and playful

F. Very alert and ready

G. I felt aggressive and very responsive

H. Smart decisions came easy

I. Felt very confident about my abilities

J. Time seemed to stop

K. It was fun and I looked at every problem as a challenge

L. I didn't want it to end

"Great competitors do not play well under pressure . . . Skillful competitors perform well in pressure situations because of their ability to eliminate pressure."

Jim E. Loehr

Five Fundamentals of Mental Toughness for Golf

by Dr. James Loehr, LGE, Sports Science, Inc.

FUNDAMENTAL ONE:
IDEAL PERFORMANCE STATE AWARENESS

How do you feel when you are playing your best? Take inventory of all areas of play and ask yourself the Four Questions:

- Did I give 100% effort?

- Am I making excuses?

- Did I have a confident/fighter image?

- Was I positive and optimistic?

FUNDAMENTAL TWO:
STAGES BETWEEN SHOT MANAGEMENT SKILLS

- Reaction Stage: Immediately follows shot. How do you deal with the shot that has just been hit, good or bad?

- Recovery Sequence: Relaxation phase from one shot to the next. It is important to clear your mind of all past and future shots, and "stop and smell the flowers," converse with your fellow competitors, to just relax.

- Preparation Stage: This phase starts about twenty yards from the ball and is the beginning of the sequence to plan the next shot. During this stage you are very analytical about your shot, from checking yardage and pin placement to gauging the wind and your lie. You must be very precise in this stage and not take any calculation for granted. Be sure you have it 100% right before going to the next stage.

- Ritual Preshot Routine: Turning the shot into automatic mode, your attention is focused fully on the target as you complete the shot at hand. There should be very little or preferably no mechanical thoughts at this stage.

FUNDAMENTAL THREE:
PRACTICE VERSUS PLAY SKILLS

Taking what you have learned on the practice tee and playing with it on the course.

- Hit five balls with mechanics fully in mind, focusing on the fundamentals that need work.

- Immediately hit five balls focusing 100% on target and your precise preshot routine. Make the routine as identical as possible for every shot.

FUNDAMENTAL FOUR:
PRE-MATCH PREPARATION SKILLS

Properly preparing for competition takes organization in the areas that will specifically help you in the competitive arena.

- Practice

- Organized schedules

- Diet

- Sleep

FUNDAMENTAL FIVE:
GOLF IMAGERY SKILLS

Learning to picture yourself playing your best.

- Hitting the perfect shot

- Making swing corrections

- Picturing targets

"Winning is not a sometime thing . . . it's an all time thing!"

Vince Lombardi

List the steps you take prior to your shot below.

Preshot Routine

Establishing a preshot routine that works well and comes naturally is essential to your game.

PRESHOT ROUTINE
1.
2.
3.
4.
5.
6.
7.
8.
9.
10.

AVERAGE TIME:

COMMENTS:

" Fear is an illusion."

Michael Jordan

Preshot Routine

List the steps you take prior to your shot below.

PRESHOT ROUTINE
1.
2.
3.
4.
5.
6.
7.
8.
9.
10.

AVERAGE TIME:

COMMENTS:

List the steps you take prior to your shot below.

PRESHOT ROUTINE
1.
2.
3.
4.
5.
6.
7.
8.
9.
10.

AVERAGE TIME:

COMMENTS:

Preshot Routine

Establishing a preshot routine that works well and comes naturally is essential to your game.

Just For Today

by Dr. James Loehr, LGE, Sports Science, Inc.

JUST FOR TODAY

I will become challenged when problems come my way. Today I will be a great problem solver.

JUST FOR TODAY

I will love the battle. I can create my own state of enjoyment. I will accept the hand that is dealt to me. No complaining!

JUST FOR TODAY

I will exercise, eat, and train right. Self-discipline will bring the confidence I search for.

JUST FOR TODAY

I will take charge of how I feel. I am not at the mercy of my emotions.

JUST FOR TODAY

I will set aside some time to relax and simply let go. Relaxation is an essential part of my training.

JUST FOR TODAY

I will have a plan to follow. The plan will keep me focused and organized.

JUST FOR TODAY

I will stop saying "if I had time." If I want time, I will make it.

JUST FOR TODAY

I will find humor in my mistakes. When I can smile inside, I am in control.

JUST FOR TODAY

I will do things the best I can. I will be satisfied with what I have done.

JUST FOR TODAY

I will do the ordinary things in my training extraordinarily well. It's the little things that make the big difference.

JUST FOR TODAY

I choose to believe that I can make the difference and that I am in control of my world.

THE CHOICE IS MINE

"There is nothing either good or bad, but thinking makes it so."

William Shakespeare

Golf's Great Traditions

*"The most important thing I can tell you about Arnold and myself is,
regardless of anything that might have divided us over the years, both of
us believe with everything that's in us in the traditions of the game."*

JACK NICKLAUS

Golfing Etiquette

Never play a shot until you are sure that no one will be in the tee in which your ball might possibly go. Also make sure that no one will be in the area of your swing. If you should hit a shot that appears to have any chance of striking somebody, immediately yell "FORE" as loudly as possible. If someone yells "fore," do not look in that direction but instead drop to your knees facing away from the sound, duck your head, and cover the back of your head with your hands.

Never move ahead of a player who is about to play. When you are done with a hole, move away from the green to the next tee as quickly as possible. Never mark your scorecard on or next to the green.

The player who had the honor should be allowed to play before another player tees his ball. No one should move, talk, or stand directly behind the ball or the hole when a player is addressing the ball or making a stroke.

Players should play without undue delay. No group should fall one full hole behind the group ahead of it. If it should do so, it should step aside, motion the following group to play through, and not resume play until that group is safely out of range. No group can play faster than the slowest group ahead of it.

When searching for a ball, as soon as it becomes obvious that it will not easily be found, signal the following group to play through.

Care should be taken not to injure the green or the cup in removing, laying down, picking up, or replacing the flagstick. All cleat scuffs made by a player should be immediately repaired. Spike marks left by other players should be repaired, as a courtesy, after playing the hole. When removing a ball from the cup, stand as far from the hole as possible.

After playing from a bunker, all marks left in the bunker should be carefully smoothed or raked. Rakes for this purpose are either placed next to the bunkers or carried in the player's cart.

Through the green, all divot holes made by the player should be immediately repaired. On bent turf, the cut turf is replaced and stepped down. On bermuda turf, the hole should be filled with sand if the cart carries a sand bucket. If not, the divot hole should be kicked in from the sides and smoothed.

On the green, all ball marks should be immediately repaired using either a tee or a special divot repair tool.

Golf carts should never be driven onto a tee or a green or onto the banks of either. Whenever near the tee or green, keep the cart on the cart path if one is available. In wet weather conditions, special rules regarding cart movement may be imposed. If using a cart, always check with the golf shop or the starter to find out if any such restrictions apply.

Like motorized carts, pullcarts should not be pulled up the slopes leading to tees or greens.

The golf bag should never be placed on the teeing ground or on the green.

Golf is a game of courtesy. Prior to teeing off, it is customary to shake the hand of your fellow competitor or opponent and wish him "good luck." After the round, the hand should be shaken again, and the player thanked for the game. If the player has played well, it is customary to congratulate him on his performance.

Practice What You Preach

When Arnold Palmer won the Open Championship at Royal Birkdale in 1961, he had a seven at one hole when there was not another person present who did not think it had been a six. As he had prepared to recover from a bunker, Palmer's ball moved fractionally. Only he was aware of it, knowing too that it was a penalty stroke. He called it at once. But the gods have a habit of rewarding virtue. Palmer still won his first British Open, by a stroke.

"The quality of a person's life is in direct proportion to [his] commitment to excellence."

Vince Lombardi

Course Strategy

"The only unplayable lie I can think of is when you're supposed
to be playing golf and come home with lipstick on your collar."

ARNOLD PALMER

Course Strategy

ARNIE'S PHILOSOPHY

Playing great golf is more than just ball-striking—it's scoring. How well you score greatly depends on how well you put all of your individual skills and abilities to work at once and attack a course. Every player, regardless of skill level, should always have a clear-cut strategy, or plan, in mind on how they would like to play a particular hole. It's really another type of visualization. If you have a clear plan in mind, you'll often be successful, or at least come close. But to fire away without a plan means the ball can finish literally anywhere.

Strategy can be broken down into three basic categories. The first I call "go for broke" because it's a very aggressive style of play, where you take a lot of risks for the sake of scoring.

The second type of strategy is just the opposite. I call it "bailing out," because it avoids potential trouble at all costs, sometimes to the point of hitting away from the green.

The third strategy I've labeled "playing safe." It's basically a combination of the first two. A fair amount of risk is involved in playing the course but so is a fair amount of caution.

MATCHING YOUR STRATEGY TO YOUR SKILLS

The most important factor in choosing a playing strategy is to pick one that fits both your golfing ability and your playing personality.

All of us would agree that an excellent strategy on most par-four holes would be to crack a 280-yard drive down the middle of the fairway, knock the ball close to the pin with a short iron and make birdie. But how many players can realistically expect to do this? "You dance with who you brung," they say in the South, meaning you must match your strategy to your skills.

There's no rule in golf that says you have to hit the driver or even a 3-wood off the tee. The key to golf is to play the ball to the best position from which to play the next shot. Where you place the ball off the tee is usually more important than how far you hit it. Shooting for the pin may also seem heroic, but if the percentages are so high against you, what's the point?

RISKS VERSUS GAMBLING

Poor decisions are the greatest cause of most high scores by weekend golfers. Further, they make these bad decisions, I feel, because they really don't understand the difference between taking a risk and taking a gamble.

A risk is when I know I can play the shot required, say, nine times out of ten, yet there are certain hazards present that may cost me a penalty if I don't pull off the shot as planned.

A shot becomes a gamble when I'm just hoping I can play it. If my chances of a successful execution are only one in ten, I'd be better off playing safe or even bailing out to avoid a disaster.

Despite my reputation as a go-for-broke player, I never have tried a shot in a tournament that I wasn't sure I could make. That's the crucial difference. Too many amateurs take gambles while expecting to make career shots.

CONFIDENCE

There is one key to maximizing your chances of making the shot when a risk is involved, and it's having confidence in your ability to play it. If you're confident in your ability to perform the task, then your mind will be filled with images of the fine shot you're about to play. This image then will block the hazards present out of your mind and allow you to put a good, accelerating stroke on the ball.

"GOING FOR BROKE" IN THE 1960 U.S. OPEN

There have been a lot of times when I used the "go for broke" strategy in tournament competition, but the time where it paid off most was in the final round of the 1960 U.S. Open at Cherry Hills Country Club.

Starting out seven strokes behind leader Mike Souchak, I knew I couldn't be timid if I wanted any chance at winning. I had to attack the course.

On the par-four first hole, I successfully attempted to drive the green to make birdie. I chipped in from thirty-five feet on the second hole for another birdie. On the par-four third my drive was just short of the green and I chipped to a foot away for another birdie, then wedged to within eighteen feet on the fourth and sank the putt for my fourth consecutive birdie. A par on the fifth was followed by a twenty-five foot putt for a deuce on the 174 yard par-three sixth and a six foot putt for a sixth birdie on the par-four seventh hole.

My strategy had worked: six birdies in seven holes and a front nine score of 30 had put me right in the thick of things. But the day wasn't over yet, since the back nine at Cherry Hills is a tough test. I played steadily the rest of the way for a solid two-under par 35 on the back for a score of 65 and the U.S. Open crown.

DEVELOPING YOUR OWN STRATEGY

Every player should make a rule to have some kind of strategy in mind on every hole he plays before ever taking a swing. Don't just tee off without some type of goal in mind and a game plan to achieve it.

Sure, things won't always work out exactly as planned. You'll be surprised, though, at how much more confident you'll feel when addressing the ball on the tee when you have a good idea of where you want to hit it and why; instead of just swinging away.

Remember, tailor your strategy to your game. It would be nice always to play for birdie, but there are many of you who would be happy to score a bogey on most difficult holes. If that's the case, then play a strategy to do just that. Plan on taking three shots to reach the green on a par four instead of forcing to make it in two. Concentrate on using the clubs you feel most comfortable with and save the others for the practice tee.

Think. Always remember to think before hitting any shot. Remember the old saying about golf being 90% mental? Well, strategy is the area where most of that mental work needs to be done.

"If one advances confidently in the direction of his dreams, and endeavors to live the life which he had imagined, he will meet with success unexpected in common hours."

Henry David Thoreau

HOLE #	STRATEGY
1	
2	
3	
4	
5	
6	
7	
8	
9	
10	
11	
12	
13	
14	
15	
16	
17	
18	

Course Strategy Notes

For courses that you play repeatedly, note successful strategies or tactics to use on each hole.

_____

Golf Course

_____

Date

COMMENTS:

_____

_____

_____

_____

_____

_____

_____

_____

Course Strategy Notes

_____

Golf Course

_____

Date

HOLE #	STRATEGY
1	
2	
3	
4	
5	
6	
7	
8	
9	
10	
11	
12	
13	
14	
15	
16	
17	
18	

COMMENTS:

_____

_____

_____

_____

_____

_____

_____

_____

_____

HOLE #	STRATEGY
1	
2	
3	
4	
5	
6	
7	
8	
9	
10	
11	
12	
13	
14	
15	
16	
17	
18	

Course Strategy Notes

For courses that you play repeatedly, note successful strategies or tactics to use on each hole.

_____

Golf Course

_____

Date

COMMENTS:

Course Strategy Notes

Golf Course

Date

HOLE #	STRATEGY
1	
2	
3	
4	
5	
6	
7	
8	
9	
10	
11	
12	
13	
14	
15	
16	
17	
18	

COMMENTS:

HOLE #	STRATEGY
1	
2	
3	
4	
5	
6	
7	
8	
9	
10	
11	
12	
13	
14	
15	
16	
17	
18	

Course Strategy Notes

For courses that you play repeatedly, note successful strategies or tactics to use on each hole.

Golf Course

Date

COMMENTS:

Your Clubs

"Speak softly and carry a big stick; you will go far."

Theodore Roosevelt

Club Fitting

Getting the most out of your clubs depends on how well you are able to hit with them.

Be sure to have them individually fitted to your specifications.

Keep a record of how your clubs have been fitted.

WHAT YOU NOW HAVE

	SET LENGTH	LIE	STATIC WEIGHT	SWING WEIGHT	GRIP SIZE	SHAFT MATERIAL	SHAFT FLEX	LOFT	FACE ANGLE	OTHER
IRONS	___	___	___	___	___	___	___	___	___	___
WOODS	___	___	___	___	___	___	___	___	___	___

CONDITION:
_____
_____
_____

RECOMMENDATIONS
_____
_____
_____

	SET LENGTH	LIE	STATIC WEIGHT	SWING WEIGHT	GRIP SIZE	SHAFT MATERIAL	SHAFT FLEX	LOFT	FACE ANGLE	OTHER
IRONS	___	___	___	___	___	___	___	___	___	___

| 1 | 2 | 3 | 4 | 5 | 6 | 7 | 8 | 9 | PW | SW |

	SET LENGTH	LIE	STATIC WEIGHT	SWING WEIGHT	GRIP SIZE	SHAFT MATERIAL	SHAFT FLEX	LOFT	FACE ANGLE	OTHER
WOODS	___	___	___	___	___	___	___	___	___	___

| 1 | 2 | 3 | 4 | 5 | 6 | 7 |

REGRIP _____

RESHAFT _____

REFINISH _____

OTHER COMMENTS _____
_____
_____

Club Fitting

WHAT YOU NOW HAVE

	SET LENGTH	LIE	STATIC WEIGHT	SWING WEIGHT	GRIP SIZE	SHAFT MATERIAL	SHAFT FLEX	LOFT	FACE ANGLE	OTHER
IRONS	___	___	___	___	___	___	___	___	___	___
WOODS	___	___	___	___	___	___	___	___	___	___

CONDITION:

_____

_____

_____

RECOMMENDATIONS

_____

_____

_____

	SET LENGTH	LIE	STATIC WEIGHT	SWING WEIGHT	GRIP SIZE	SHAFT MATERIAL	SHAFT FLEX	LOFT	FACE ANGLE	OTHER
IRONS	___	___	___	___	___	___	___	___	___	___

| 1 | 2 | 3 | 4 | 5 | 6 | 7 | 8 | 9 | PW | SW |

	SET LENGTH	LIE	STATIC WEIGHT	SWING WEIGHT	GRIP SIZE	SHAFT MATERIAL	SHAFT FLEX	LOFT	FACE ANGLE	OTHER
WOODS	___	___	___	___	___	___	___	___	___	___

| 1 | 2 | 3 | 4 | 5 | 6 | 7 |

REGRIP _____

RESHAFT _____

REFINISH _____

OTHER COMMENTS

_____

_____

Golf Club Distance Calibration Chart

For each club, enter the length (in yards) for each of six attempts.

The average is a personal calibration for distance for that club.

Update your calibrations periodically if you replace clubs or purchase new ones.

———————

Date

CLUB	FIRST ATTEMPT	SECOND ATTEMPT	THIRD ATTEMPT	FOURTH ATTEMPT	FIFTH ATTEMPT	SIXTH ATTEMPT	AVERAGE (YDS)
			LENGTH (YDS)				
SW							
SW2							
PW							
9							
8							
7							
6							
5							
4							
3							
2							
1							
7 WOOD							
6 WOOD							
5 WOOD							
4 WOOD							
3 WOOD							
2 WOOD							
DRIVER							

NOTES & GOALS

———————————————————————————————
———————————————————————————————
———————————————————————————————
———————————————————————————————
———————————————————————————————
———————————————————————————————
———————————————————————————————

Golf Club Distance Calibration Chart

_____

Date

CLUB	FIRST ATTEMPT	SECOND ATTEMPT	LENGTH (YDS) THIRD ATTEMPT	FOURTH ATTEMPT	FIFTH ATTEMPT	SIXTH ATTEMPT	AVERAGE (YDS)
SW							
SW2							
PW							
9							
8							
7							
6							
5							
4							
3							
2							
1							
7 WOOD							
6 WOOD							
5 WOOD							
4 WOOD							
3 WOOD							
2 WOOD							
DRIVER							

NOTES & GOALS

_____

_____

_____

_____

_____

_____

_____

Golf Club Distance Calibration Chart

For each club, enter the length (in yards) for each of six attempts.

The average is a personal calibration for distance for that club.

Update your calibrations periodically if you replace clubs or purchase new ones.

_____

Date

CLUB	FIRST ATTEMPT	SECOND ATTEMPT	THIRD ATTEMPT	FOURTH ATTEMPT	FIFTH ATTEMPT	SIXTH ATTEMPT	AVERAGE (YDS)
			LENGTH (YDS)				
SW							
SW2							
PW							
9							
8							
7							
6							
5							
4							
3							
2							
1							
7 WOOD							
6 WOOD							
5 WOOD							
4 WOOD							
3 WOOD							
2 WOOD							
DRIVER							

NOTES & GOALS

_____

_____

_____

_____

_____

_____

_____

_____

Average Golf Club Distance Calibration Chart

CLUB	18 HANDICAP		9 HANDICAP		TOUR PROFESSIONAL	
	M	W	M	W	M	W
SW (60°)	65	40	80	55	90	80
SW	85	60	100	70	105	95
PW	100	70	115	80	120	105
9	115	75	125	95	135	120
8	125	85	135	105	150	130
7	135	90	145	115	160	140
6	145	100	155	125	170	150
5	155	110	165	135	180	160
4	165	120	175	150	190	170
3	175	130	185	160	200	180
2	185	–	195	170	210	190
1	195	–	205	–	220	200
7 wood	165	100	185	140	200	175
6 wood	170	110	195	150	205	180
5 wood	175	120	200	160	210	190
4 wood	185	130	210	170	220	200
3 wood	195	140	215	180	230	210
2 wood	205	145	225	185	245	225
DRIVER	215	150	235	190	260	235

U.S.G.A. Yardages for Guidance

PAR	MEN	WOMEN
3	up to 250 yards	up to 210 yards
4	251-470 yards	211-400 yards
5	471 and over	401-575 yards
6		576 and over

Golf Statistical Averages

CATEGORY	18 HANDICAP	9 HANDICAP	TOUR PROFESSIONAL
Driving Distance	215	235	261
Fairways	6	7.5	9.5
Greens	5	9	12
Putts	38	34	29
Sand Saves	12%	27%	50%
Average Penalty Shots	4	2.5	.5
Scoring Average	90	80	71.10

C H A P T E R **8**

Golf Scores and Stats

"The golf ball doesn't appreciate that you're a hot shot player, nor does the course. It's a clean sheet every time you play, and you have to impress them with your talent all over again."

ARNOLD PALMER

Scores and Stats

Write down your own scores and stats.

Periodically average your stats. Then you can compare them to the average stats of the comparable tour (PGA, LPGA, Senior, Nike) or your favorite professional golfer.

DATE	COURSE	PAR	WEATHER CONDITIONS
	YOUR AVERAGE:		
	TOUR AVERAGE:		

SCORE	FAIRWAYS	GREENS	PUTTS	SAND SAVES	SUMMARY

Scores and Stats

Write down your own scores and stats.

Periodically average your stats. Then you can compare them to the average stats of the comparable tour (PGA, LPGA, Senior, Nike) or your favorite professional golfer.

DATE	COURSE	PAR	WEATHER CONDITIONS
	YOUR AVERAGE:		
	TOUR AVERAGE:		

SCORE	FAIRWAYS	GREENS	PUTTS	SAND SAVES	SUMMARY

Scores and Stats

Write down your own scores and stats.

Periodically average your stats. Then you can compare them to the average stats of the comparable tour (PGA, LPGA, Senior, Nike) or your favorite professional golfer.

DATE	COURSE	PAR	WEATHER CONDITIONS
YOUR AVERAGE:			
TOUR AVERAGE:			

SCORE	FAIRWAYS	GREENS	PUTTS	SAND SAVES	SUMMARY

Scores and Stats

Write down your own scores and stats.

Periodically average your stats. Then you can compare them to the average stats of the comparable tour (PGA, LPGA, Senior, Nike) or your favorite professional golfer.

DATE	COURSE	PAR	WEATHER CONDITIONS
	YOUR AVERAGE:		
	TOUR AVERAGE:		

SCORE	FAIRWAYS	GREENS	PUTTS	SAND SAVES	SUMMARY

Planning Calendar

"Plan your work for today and every day, then work your plan."

NORMAN VINCENT PEALE

Year-at-a-Glance Golf Planning Calendar

Note your upcoming lessons, games, and tournaments for the whole year.

JANUARY	FEBRUARY	MARCH
_____	_____	_____
_____	_____	_____
_____	_____	_____
_____	_____	_____
_____	_____	_____
_____	_____	_____
_____	_____	_____
_____	_____	_____
_____	_____	_____
_____	_____	_____
_____	_____	_____
_____	_____	_____
_____	_____	_____
_____	_____	_____
_____	_____	_____
_____	_____	_____
_____	_____	_____
_____	_____	_____
_____	_____	_____
_____	_____	_____
_____	_____	_____
_____	_____	_____

APRIL	MAY	JUNE

Year-at-a-Glance Golf Planning Calendar

Year-at-a-Glance Golf Planning Calendar

JULY	AUGUST	SEPTEMBER
_____	_____	_____
_____	_____	_____
_____	_____	_____
_____	_____	_____
_____	_____	_____
_____	_____	_____
_____	_____	_____
_____	_____	_____
_____	_____	_____
_____	_____	_____
_____	_____	_____
_____	_____	_____
_____	_____	_____
_____	_____	_____
_____	_____	_____
_____	_____	_____
_____	_____	_____
_____	_____	_____
_____	_____	_____
_____	_____	_____
_____	_____	_____
_____	_____	_____
_____	_____	_____
_____	_____	_____
_____	_____	_____
_____	_____	_____
_____	_____	_____

OCTOBER	NOVEMBER	DECEMBER

Year-at-a-Glance Golf Planning Calendar

Photos & Memories

*"I'd rather win one tournament in my entire
life than make the cut every week."*

Arnold Palmer

Scrapbook

*For Photographs
and Clippings*

PHOTO HERE

GOLF PARTNERS

_____

_____

_____

_____

_____

_____

_____

_____

Scrapbook

CLIPPINGS HERE

Scrapbook

For Photographs and Clippings

PHOTO HERE

PHOTO HERE

Scrapbook

CLIPPINGS HERE

Scrapbook

*For Photographs
and Clippings*

Scrapbook

CLIPPINGS HERE

Scrapbook

*For Photographs
and Clippings*

Scrapbook

CLIPPINGS HERE

Best Golf Holes

Record the date, course, and details of your best shots, including holes-in-one.

DATE
_____

COURSE
_____

COMMENTS
_____
_____
_____
_____

DATE
_____

COURSE
_____

COMMENTS
_____
_____
_____
_____

SCORECARD FROM
_____

Best Golf Holes

DATE _____

COURSE _____

COMMENTS _____

_____

_____

_____

_____

DATE _____

COURSE _____

COMMENTS _____

_____

_____

_____

SCORECARD FROM _____

Best Golf Holes

Record the date, course, and details of your best shots, including holes-in-one.

DATE

COURSE

COMMENTS

DATE

COURSE

COMMENTS

SCORECARD FROM

DATE _____

COURSE _____

COMMENTS _____

_____

_____

_____

_____

DATE _____

COURSE _____

COMMENTS _____

_____

_____

_____

_____

Best Golf Holes

SCORECARD FROM _____

Best Golf Holes

Record the date, course, and details of your best shots, including holes-in-one.

DATE

COURSE

COMMENTS

DATE

COURSE

COMMENTS

SCORECARD FROM

Best Golf Holes

DATE _____

COURSE _____

COMMENTS _____

_____

_____

_____

_____

DATE _____

COURSE _____

COMMENTS _____

_____

_____

_____

_____

SCORECARD FROM _____

Best Golf Holes

Record the date, course, and details of your best shots, including holes-in-one.

DATE
_____

COURSE
_____

COMMENTS
_____
_____
_____
_____

DATE
_____

COURSE
_____

COMMENTS
_____
_____
_____
_____

SCORECARD FROM
_____

Best Golf Holes

DATE
_____

COURSE
_____

COMMENTS
_____
_____
_____
_____

DATE
_____

COURSE
_____

COMMENTS
_____
_____
_____
_____

SCORECARD FROM
_____

Best Golf Holes

Record the date, course, and details of your best shots, including holes-in-one.

DATE _____

COURSE _____

COMMENTS _____

_____

_____

_____

DATE _____

COURSE _____

COMMENTS _____

_____

_____

_____

SCORECARD FROM _____

Best Golf Holes

DATE _____

COURSE _____

COMMENTS _____

_____

_____

_____

DATE _____

COURSE _____

COMMENTS _____

_____

_____

_____

SCORECARD FROM _____

Golf Terms

ADDRESSING THE BALL

Taking a stance and grounding the club (except in a hazard) before taking a swing.

APPROACH

A shot to the putting green.

APRON

Grass area (fringe) immediately surrounding the putting surface.

AWAY

Ball furthest from the hole; to be played first.

BIRDIE

One stroke under the designated par of a hole.

BOGEY

Usually one stroke over the designated par of a hole.

BUNKER

A hazard, often a depression, usually covered with sand (frequently referred to as a sand trap). Grass bordering or within a bunker is not considered part of a hazard.

CASUAL WATER

A temporary water accumulation not intended as hazard.

DIVOT

Turf displaced by player's club when making a swing.

DOG-LEG

A hole in which the route of play angles to the right or left before reaching the putting surface.

DOWN

The number of holes (match play) or strokes (stroke play) a player is behind an opponent.

EAGLE

Two strokes under par for a hole.

FAIRWAY

Closely mowed route of play between teeing area and putting green.

FLAGSTICK

A thin, movable pole with a flag attached at the top, centered in the hole of the putting green to indicate its location. Also called pin.

FORE

A warning cry to any person in the way of play.

FORECADDIE

A person assigned to indicate to players the position of balls on the course.

GREEN

The putting surface.

GROSS SCORE

Total number of strokes taken to complete a designated round.

GROUND

Touching the surface of the ground with the sole of the club at address.

HANDICAP

A deduction from a player's gross score devised to match his score against par and to equate differential abilities of other players.

HALVED

Competitive term used to indicate identical scores on a hole.

HAZARD

A term used to designate bunkers (sand traps) or water areas.

HONOR

The right to tee off first, earned by scoring lowest on preceding hole.

HOOK

A stroke made by a right-handed player which curves the ball to the left of the target. For the left-handed player, the ball will curve to the right.

HOSEL

Extension of the clubhead into which the shaft fits.

LIE

Stationary position of the ball in the grass or sand; also, the angle of the shaft in relation to the ground when the club sole rests naturally.

LOOSE IMPEDIMENT

A natural object, not stationary, growing or adhering to the ball, such as a leaf, twig, branch or the like.

MARKER

A person who keeps score. Tee markers define the forward limits of the teeing area.

BALL MARKER

A small coin or object used to spot a ball position on the green.

MATCH PLAY

Type of competition in which each hole is a separate contest. The winner is the player or side that wins more holes than there are left to play.

NASSAU

Competition, either match or stroke play, which awards 1 point for back nine and 1 point for total 18 holes.

NET SCORE

Gross score, less handicap.

OBSTRUCTION

In general, an artificial object erected, placed, or left on the course.

PAR

A numerical standard of scoring excellence per hole, based on yardage and two putts per green.

PROVISIONAL BALL

A second ball hit before a player looks for his original ball which apparently is out-of-bounds or lost outside a water hazard.

PULL

A straight shot in which the flight of a ball is left of the target. For a left-handed player, the flight is right of the target.

PUSH

A straight shot in which the flight of the ball is right of the target. For a left-handed player, the ball is left of the target.

ROUGH

Areas, usually, of relatively long grass, adjacent to the tee, fairway, green or hazards.

SLICE

A stroke made by a right-handed player which curves the ball to the right of the intended target. For a left-handed player, the ball will curve to the left.

STANCE

Position of the feet when addressing the ball.

STROKE

Any forward motion of the clubhead made with intent to strike the ball.

STROKE PLAY

Competition based on total number of strokes taken.

TARGET

The spot or area to which the ball is intended to land or roll.

TEE

A peg on top of which the ball is placed before striking it from the teeing area. Also, the teeing area itself.

TOP

To hit the ball above its center.

UP

The number of holes (match play) or strokes (stroke play) a player leads his opponent.

"We cherish that which has been most difficult to obtain."

Anonymous

Test Your Golf Knowledge

RULES OF GOLF

1. Outside of a hazard, a player has addressed his ball when he has done what two things?

2. Is a grass covered mound in the center of a bunker considered to be a part of the bunker?

3. Where may "casual water" occur?

    a. On the tee
    b. In the fairway
    c. In a bunker
    d. In the rough
    e. In a water hazard
    f. In a lateral water hazard
    g. On the green
    h. Out of bounds

4. True or false: A "fellow competitor" is a contestant in a stroke play tournament or any contestant other than the player or his opponent in a match play tournament.

5. Which of the following are considered to be a part of a player's "equipment"?

    a. A player's golf shoes
    b. A player's ball lying in the fairway
    c. A player's ball marker when the ball is marked on the green
    d. A player's clubs
    e. A player's cart that he is driving
    f. A tee in the ground used by the player to measure the extent of his drop area

6. Which of the following are considered "ground under repair"?

    a. An unmarked pile of grass clippings left to decay in the rough

    b. An unmarked bare area in the middle of the fairway

    c. An unmarked hole in the rough where a dead tree has been removed

    d. An unmarked concrete cart path

    e. White-lined areas

    f. Aeration holes

    g. A hole left where a hazard stake has been removed

7. Which of the following are hazards?

    a. A sand trap

    b. A large tree in the middle of the fairway

    c. A lake in front of the green

    d. A grass bunker

    e. A swamp paralleling the hole

8. By convention, match each markings with the area it defines.

    a. Red stakes   1. Out of bounds

    b. White stakes   2. Lateral hazard

    c. White lines   3. Water hazard

    d. Yellow stakes   4. Ground under repair

9. Which of the following are classified as loose impediments in the fairway?

    a. A soda can

    b. A dead leaf on the ground

    c. Dew

    d. A clump of sand

    e. A tree limb lying loose on the ground

    f. A tree limb lying on the ground which is attached to the tree

    g. A worm

10. When is a golf ball "officially lost"?

   a. When it is not found after five minutes of searching

   b. When the ball is found within five minutes of searching but can not be positively identified

   c. When the player declares the ball to be lost

   d. When the player puts a provisional ball in play

   e. When a player plays a provisional ball from the area where his original ball is likely to be

   f. When the player plays a provisional ball without announcing that it is a provisional

11. Which of the following are classified as "obstructions"?

   a. Boundary stakes

   b. Hazard stakes

   c. A cement cart path

   d. A piece of construction lumber

   e. A tree limb detached from the tree

   f. An iron post on a ball washer

   g. An iron post on a bird bath just out of bounds

12. A ball is on the putting green if:

   a. Any part of the ball touches the green

   b. No part of the ball touches the fringe

   c. Part of the ball overhangs the green, even though none of the ball touches it

13. The "stroke" begins when:

   a. The ball is addressed

   b. The club begins the backswing

   c. The club begins the downswing

   d. The club contacts the ball

14. "Through the green" includes which of the following?

    a. The teeing ground of the hole being played

    b. All teeing grounds on the course

    c. The fairway of the hole being played

    d. All fairways on the course

    e. All hazards on the course

    f. The green of the hole being played

    g. All greens but the one being played

    h. All the rough

15. A player leaves a putt hanging on the lip of the hole. He steps heavily near the ball and it falls into the hole. Is he penalized?

16. Which of the following are legal?

    a. A screw in the sole plate of a wood that will come out and allow for the insertion of weights

    b. A driver grip with a flat spot for the thumbs

    c. A two-sided chipper with a 5-iron loft

    d. An iron groove too wide due to excess wear

    e. Replacing a club broken in anger

    f. Vaseline applied to a driver face

    g. A driver grip with an imprinted dot indicating where the thumbs should go

17. The player hits a greenside bunker shot. The ball splits in two. The bigger piece falls into the hole, the smaller piece flies out of bounds. What happens now?

"I will prepare and someday my chance will come."
Abraham Lincoln

18. Which are the scoring responsibilities of a player with respect to his own card?

    a. Making sure each hole is recorded correctly

    b. Making sure that both nine and eighteen hole totals are correct

    c. Checking to be sure his marker has signed the card

    d. Signing the card when correct

    e. Returning the card to the officials as soon as possible

19. If you sign and return a card with a six on a hole where you made a five, what score will you receive on that hole?

20. A player has the honor on the tee but hooks his drive into a clump of trees. If he wishes to play a provisional ball, when will he play it?

21. Which of the following statements are true?

    a. Part of the ball and part of the players stance must be within the teeing ground when teeing off

    b. Only part of the players ball must be within the teeing ground when teeing off

    c. A player may not move one of the tee markers when teeing off if he wishes to stand where the marker is

    d. If a ball falls off the tee in the act of addressing it, the player lies one and the ball may be reteed

    e. If a ball falls off the tee in the act of addressing it, the player lies one and the ball must be played as it lies

    f. If a ball falls off the tee in the act of addressing it, the player lies zero and must play the ball where it lies

22. When addressing a ball in a water hazard, may the players club be allowed to touch grass and weeds growing behind the ball?

23. A player may be penalized for playing a wrong ball from which areas of the course?

    a. Fairway

    b. Bunkers

    c. Rough

    d. Water hazards

    e. Lateral hazards

    f. Out of bounds

    g. Green

24. In stroke play, a player marks his ball on the first green, puts it in his pocket, then pulls out a different ball and holes out with it. The mistake is not discovered until the second green. What is the ruling?

    a. No penalty

    b. Score stands with a two shot penalty

    c. Two shot penalty, return to first green and hole out with correct ball

    d. Disqualification

25. A player whiffs his tee shot, then pushes the ball and tee lower into the ground. He swings again and hooks that ball out of bounds. He tees up another ball and hits it down the fairway. What does he lie now?

Answers can be found on page 129.

Answers can be found on page 129.

"It is a mistake to look too far ahead. Only one link in the chain of destiny can be handled at a time."

Winston Churchill

GOLF HISTORY

1. What two teams play for the Ryder Cup?

2. What is the governing body for golf in the United States?

3. Where was golf's first official hole?

4. What four tournaments make up golf's Grand Slam?

5. What was one of the first golf balls made of?

6. When was the first British Open held?

7. What was the first country outside of Great Britain to play golf?

8. When was the PGA Senior Tour officially born?

9. What year was the Women's Golf Association formed?

10. What grip revolutionized golf in 1905?

11. How many golf balls are there on the moon?

12. What year was the Professional Golfers Association founded?

13. What state has 3,611 miles of golf?

14. What is the only major tournament Arnold Palmer never won?

15. How many "green jackets" does Arnold Palmer own?

16. What year did Arnold Palmer win the first of his four Masters Tournaments?

17. What international sports management group started with Arnold Palmer?

18. What was Arnold Palmer's lowest competitive round?

19. In what years did Arnold Palmer win the PGA money title?

20. Where did Arnold Palmer attend college?

Answers can be found on page 129.

NAMES IN THE GAME

1. Who was the first player to win the US Open and the US Amateur in the same year?

2. What golf accessory was patented by George Grant on December 12, 1899?

3. Who completed the Grand Slam by winning the US Open, US Amateur, British Open and British Amateur?

4. Who made a double eagle at the Masters in 1935, regarded as one of the most famous shots in the history of the game?

5. Who was the first US woman to win the British Ladies Championship?

6. Who won the 1950 US Open 15 months after almost being killed in an automobile-bus accident?

7. Who was the first woman golfer to win $1,000,000?

8. What golfers were known as the big three?

9. What golfer is nicknamed "The Shark"?

10. Who won the 1913 US Open as an amateur?

11. Who holds the record for consecutive PGA Tour victories?

12. Who was hanged in 1637 for stealing two golf balls?

13. Who coined the term "yips"?

14. Who is considered the father of American golf?

15. Who was the first American to win the British Open?

Answers can be found on page 130.

Answers

RULES OF GOLF

1. Taken his stance and grounded his club.
2. No
3. a, b, c, d & g
4. False
5. a, d & e
6. c, e & g
7. a, c & e
8. (a-2) (b-1) (c-4) (d-3)
9. b, e & g
10. a, e & f
11. b, c, d & f
12. a, b
13. c
14. c, d, g & h
15. Yes
16. a, d & g
17. The stroke is canceled. The player replays the shot with a different ball, and no penalty is involved.
18. a, c, d & e
19. Six
20. After his playing partner.
21. b & c
22. Yes
23. a, c & g
24. b
25. Six (1-Whiff, 2-Moving ball in play, 3-Failure to replace, 4-Hook, 5-Out of bounds penalty, 6-Drive in fairway)

GOLF HISTORY

1. USA and Europe
2. United States Golf Association
3. St. Andrews
4. Masters, PGA, US Open, British Open
5. Leather strips and goose feathers

6. 1860 in Scotland
7. India
8. 1980
9. 1897
10. The Vardon Grip-explained by Harry Vardon in *The Complete Golfer*, 1905
11. 3
12. 1916
13. Florida
14. PGA
15. 4
16. 1958
17. IMG
18. 62, 1959 Thunderbird Invitational (fourth round), 1966 Los Angeles Open (third round)
19. 1958, 60, 62, 63
20. Wake Forest

NAMES IN THE GAME

1. Chick Evans, 1916
2. The golf tee
3. Bobby Jones, 1930
4. Gene Sarazen
5. Babe Didrickson-Zaharias, 1947
6. Ben Hogan
7. Kathy Whitworth
8. Palmer, Player, Nicklaus
9. Greg Norman
10. Francis Quimet
11. Byron Nelson
12. Francis Brown
13. Tommy Armour
14. John Reid
15. Walter Hagen

Arnold Palmer Golf Academy

At the Arnold Palmer Golf Academy, students of all ages and abilities are taught the winning philosophies behind a strong golf game. Mr. Palmer's hand-picked staff focuses on teaching the basics: swing fundamentals, scoring zone, practice, and course strategy. Instructors encourage players to enhance their own natural style by working with their current skills, not by forcing new technique.

Leading the talented group of teaching professionals is Dick Tiddy. Dick's golfing career spans over forty years of playing, teaching, and promoting the game. He was recently named to *Golf Magazine's* Top 100 Golf Instructors list and was the North Florida Section PGA Professional of the Year in 1992. He has coached Payne Stewart, Lou Holtz, Sarah Ingram, and many other well-known players.

Director Brad Brewer brings instructional, playing, and management strengths to his role at the Academy. A twelve-year veteran, Brad worked closely with Mr. Palmer to develop Academy teaching methods and instructor certification. He also writes articles for golf publications, has won sixteen professional golf competitions, and is regularly featured on the Golf Channel.

Pat Gorman brings a diverse playing background along with excellent motivational skills and trouble shot strategy to the Academy. He has taught numerous clinics, seminars, and private lessons. A graduate of the University of Wisconsin, Pat continues to compete in PGA golf competitions.

PGA member John O'Leary joined the Academy from nearby University of Central Florida. John has won several club professional events and taught many clinics, golf schools, and private lessons.

To ensure individual attention and direction the class is broken down into groups with one instructor for every four players. Rotating between the golf course and the classroom, students are able to put their lessons into action, quickly and correctly. Learning to play a better game comes easily with this aggressive, yet fun approach to golfing the Palmer way.

Arnold Palmer's Professional Career Highlights

VICTORIES

- Total 92 (US Tour 61; Foreign/International Tours 19; Senior Tour 12)

EARNINGS

- Regular PGA Tour $2,045,581
- Senior PGA Tour $1,524,719
- Foreign/International/Non-Tour US $412,008
- Total Competitive Earnings (excluding Pro-Ams & Skins Games) $3,982,308

INDIVIDUAL RECORDS

- Best 18-Hole Round: 62

    1959 Thunderbird Invitational (Fourth Round)

    1966 Los Angeles Open (Third Round)

- Lowest 72-Hole Score: 265 (64-67-64-70)

    1955 Canadian Open

- Biggest Victory Margin: 12

    1962 Phoenix Open

- Most Consecutive Birdies: 7

    Los Angeles Open (Third Round)

- Holes-in-One: 16

    Three in PGA Tour events, four on Senior PGA Tour, one in Japan, three in exhibitions, and five in miscellaneous rounds (including three at the #2 at Latrobe Country Club)

- All Time Low 18-Hole Score: 60

    Latrobe Country Club (September 1969)

AWARDS

- Charter Member, World Golf Hall of Fame, Pinehurst, North Carolina

- American Golf Hall of Fame, Foxburg, Pennsylvania

- PGA Hall of Fame, Palm Beach Gardens, Florida/ Pinehurst, North Carolina

- All American Collegiate Golf Hall of Fame, Man of the Year, 1984 Bobby Jones Award, United States Golf Association

- Herb Graffis Award, National Golf Foundation

- Associated Press Athlete of the Decade, 1960-1969

- *Sports Illustrated* Sportsman of the Year, 1960

OTHER ACHIEVEMENTS

- PGA Player of the Year, 1960 and 1962

- PGA Tour Leading Money Winner, 1958, 1960, 1962, 1963

- US Ryder Cup Team, 1961, 1963, 1965, 1967, 1971, 1973

- US Ryder Cup Captain, 1963 and 1975

Notes

Notes

Notes

Telephone Numbers

Keep a list of your favorite pro-shops, golf courses, and partners.

Arnold Palmer Golf Academy: 1-800-523-5999

_____

_____

_____

_____

_____

_____

_____

_____

_____

_____

_____

_____

_____

_____

_____

_____

_____

_____

_____

_____

_____

_____

_____

_____

_____

_____

_____

_____

_____

_____

_____

_____